Daily Ma Prompts

grade

One math prompt for every day of the school year!

- Review key math skills.
- Engage students in writing about math.
- Assess students' mathematical thinking.
- Prepare students for testing.

Written by Ann Hefflin

Managing Editor: Peggy Hambright

Editorial Team: Becky S. Andrews, Kimberley Bruck, Karen P. Shelton, Diane Badden, Thad H. McLaurin, Debra Liverman, Lauren Cox, Cindy K. Daoust, Karen A. Brudnak, Sarah Hamblet, Hope Rodgers, Dorothy C. McKinney

Production Team: Lisa K. Pitts, Pam Crane, Rebecca Saunders, Jennifer Tipton Cappoen, Chris Curry, Sarah Foreman, Theresa Lewis Goode, Clint Moore, Greg D. Rieves, Barry Slate, Donna K. Teal, Zane Williard, Tazmen Carlisle, Amy Kirtley-Hill, Cathy Edwards Simrell, Lynette Dickerson, Mark Rainey, Debbie Shoffner

www.themailbox.com

©2006 The Mailbox®
All rights reserved.
ISBN10 #1-56234-649-0 • ISBN13 #978-156234-649-2

Except as provided for herein, no part of this publication may be reproduced or transmitted in any form or by any means, electronic or mechanical, including photocopying, recording, or storing in any information storage and retrieval system or electronic online bulletin board, without prior written permission from The Education Center, Inc. Permission is given to the original purchaser to reproduce patterns and reproducibles for individual classroom use only and not for resale or distribution. Reproduction for an entire school or school system is prohibited. Please direct written inquiries to The Education Center, Inc., P.O. Box 9753, Greensboro, NC 27429-0753. The Education Center®, The Mailbox®, the mailbox/post/grass logo, and The Mailbox Book Company® are registered trademarks of The Education Center, Inc. All other brand or product names are trademarks or registered trademarks of their respective companies.

Manufactured in the United States
10 9 8 7 6 5 4 3 2

Table of Contents

How to Use This Book 2
Additional Ways to Use This Book 3
Skills Grid 4
Daily Math Prompts 5
Prompts Checklist 77
Assessment Rubric 78
Math Journal Cover 79
Math Journal Page 80

How to Use This Book

Select a Prompt

To support your math curriculum, the prompts are arranged sequentially from easier to harder skills. Begin with the first page of prompts and work your way to the last page, or use the skills grid on page 4 to help you choose prompts that best suit the needs of your students. The handy checklist on page 77 will help you keep track of the prompts you've used throughout the year.

Display the Prompt

Prompts can be displayed in many ways. Here are a few suggestions:

- Photocopy selected prompts and cut them into strips. Give one copy of a selected strip to each student or place the strips at a center.

- Make copies of a page of prompts and give one to each student at the beginning of the week.

- Copy the prompt onto the board or a piece of chart paper. Display the chart in the classroom or at a center.

- Make a transparency of the prompts to show on an overhead projector.

- If a visual is not needed, read the prompt aloud to students.

Additional Ways to Use This Book

- Use math prompts as
  - morning work
  - independent work
  - homework
  - a warm-up activity before beginning a math class
  - an activity for one math group to complete while waiting to meet with you

- Arrange students into pairs. Have each pair read and discuss the prompt before responding in writing. Or have the students in each pair complete the prompt independently and then discuss their written responses with each other.

- Take a quick assessment of your students' mathematical thinking by using the assessment rubric on page 78.

- Casually talk with individual students about their prompts to get a deeper insight into their mathematical thinking.

- Create individual student math journals by stapling a copy of the math journal cover (page 79) atop a supply of notebook paper. Or, if desired, use copies of the journal page (page 80) instead of notebook paper. Math journals are a great way to keep a running record of students' mathematical thinking and writing.

Skills Grid

Skill	Prompt #
NUMBER AND OPERATIONS	
Number and Quantitative Reasoning	
number sense	1, 3, 6, 8
expanded notation	16
place value	2, 7, 13, 17
comparing	12
comparing and ordering numbers	11
rounding	18
Addition and Subtraction	
two-digit column addition	23, 26
three-digit addition	27, 28, 31, 32
comparing addition and subtraction	39
checking subtraction	43
estimating differences	38
two-digit subtraction with regrouping	36
two-digit and three-digit subtraction with regrouping	37
three-digit subtraction	41, 42
four-digit subtraction across zeros	33
Money	
counting money	91
estimating sums of money	21, 98
adding money	97, 102
subtracting money	103, 106
adding and subtracting money	101
multiplying money	107
dividing money	108, 112
dividing and multiplying money	111
Multiplication	
comparing addition and multiplication	48
multiplication facts	62
two-digit multiplication with regrouping	52, 61
problem solving	53, 56, 57, 58
Division	
writing a division story problem	63
two-digit number divided by a one-digit number	66, 68, 71, 72
three-digit number divided by a one-digit number	67, 77, 78, 81, 82, 83
adding and dividing (finding the average)	86
problem solving	73, 76
Fractions	
parts of a whole	113, 116, 117, 118
equivalent fractions	121, 122
greatest common factor	123
comparing fractions	126, 127, 128, 133
parts of a group	131
adding like fractions	136, 138
adding mixed numbers	137, 142, 146, 147
relating fractions to real life	148
fractions as decimals	171
comparing fractions and decimals	178
fractions as decimals and percents	172
comparing fractions and percents	173
problem solving	132, 141, 143
Decimals	
writing decimals	151
relating decimals and fractions	152
comparing decimals	153, 156
comparing and ordering decimals	157
decimals as fractions	167
decimals as fractions and percents	168
rounding decimals to the nearest whole number	158
adding decimals	161
subtracting decimals	162
multiplying decimals	166
problem solving	163
Percents	
finding the percent of a number	176, 177
Problem Solving	
problem solving	22, 51, 88, 93, 96
guessing and checking	46, 47
working backward	87
making an organized list	92

Skill	Prompt #
GEOMETRY	
plane figures	25, 40
solid figures	10, 19
polygons	115, 125, 135, 145
isosceles triangle	49
circles: diameter and radius	165
similar and congruent figures	80, 90
symmetry	95, 155
lines	105
angles	60, 69
problem solving	175
MEASUREMENT	
length	9, 29, 35, 45
weight	55, 65
temperature	74
time	89, 109, 119
calendar	99
perimeter	129
area	139, 159, 179
perimeter and area	149, 169
problem solving	20
DATA ANALYSIS AND PROBABILITY	
interpreting data	5
picture graph	15, 54
line plot	30, 34
bar graph	44
circle graph	64
graphing	70, 85
range	100
mean, median, mode, and range	110
coordinate grid	120
certain, likely, and unlikely	130
possible outcomes	140
probability	150, 170
making an organized list	160
determining fairness	180
ALGEBRA	
shape patterns	4, 114
number patterns	14, 59
relationship thinking: table of data	24
input/output table	50, 79, 104
inverse operations	75
distributive property of multiplication	94
algebraic expression	124, 154
solving for x	134
writing and solving an equation	144, 164
problem solving	84, 174

NUMBER AND OPERATIONS

1. Numbers can be named in different ways. Look at some of the names for 18. Write three different ways to name the number 24. Explain your thinking.

$20 - 2 \longrightarrow \boxed{18} \longleftarrow 10 + 8$

$6 + 6 + 6$

$? \longrightarrow \boxed{24} \longleftarrow ?$ (with ? above)

NUMBER AND OPERATIONS

2. Study the number. Sally says the value of the 5 is 500. Tim thinks the value is 50. Which of them is right? Why?

7,523

NUMBER AND OPERATIONS

3. With these digits, write the largest whole number that you can. Use each digit only one time. Then write the number in words. How do you know this is the largest possible number?

2 0 7 5

ALGEBRA

4. Study the shapes. What will the next four shapes in this pattern be? Explain your answer.

△ □ □ ○ △ □ ? ? ? ?

DATA ANALYSIS AND PROBABILITY

5. Look at the table. Tell three things that the data helps you understand.

Room 12's Favorite School Days

Days	Tally Marks
Monday	|||||	
Tuesday	||
Wednesday	|||||
Thursday	|||||	
Friday	||||| |||||

Answer Key

1. Accept any expression that equals 24.
Possible answers include the following:
14 + 10, 30 – 6, and 12 x 2.

2. Sally; because the 5 is in the hundreds place.

3. 7,520; seven thousand, five hundred twenty; Explanation: Because each digit can be used only once, the largest possible number that can be written is a four-digit number with its digits written in order from greatest to least.

4. square, circle, triangle, square;
Explanation: The shapes have a repeating pattern of one triangle, two squares, and one circle.

5. Answers will vary. Possible responses include the following:
- The opinions represent 29 people.
- The favorite day is Friday.
- The least favorite day is Tuesday.
- An equal number of people like Monday and Thursday.
- Half as many people prefer Wednesday as those who prefer Friday.

NUMBER AND OPERATIONS

6. Amber rolled a die five times and got the following numbers: 6, 5, 5, 2, and 4. If she uses all five digits, what is the largest possible number she can build? What is the smallest possible number? Tell how you know.

NUMBER AND OPERATIONS

7. Write the mystery number that matches the values of the digits in the table. Explain how you got your answer.

Mystery Number

Digit	Value
9	90
4	4,000
3	300
5	50,000
4	4

NUMBER AND OPERATIONS

8. Hayley wrote the number 4,622,902 in words. Do you agree with her work? Explain how you know.

four million, six hundred twenty-two thousand, ninety-two

MEASUREMENT

9. Nick wants to use a ruler to measure his pencil. What is the pencil's length to the nearest half inch? Explain how you know.

GEOMETRY

10. Stan is stacking a set of solid figures. Which of the following figures is he more likely to be using: sphere, cube, rectangular prism, pyramid, cylinder, or cone? Explain how you know.

Answer Key

6. largest number—65,542; smallest number—24,556; Explanation: In the largest number, the digits are ordered from greatest to least. In the smallest number, the digits are ordered from least to greatest.

7. 54,394

8. No. The correct word form is four million, six hundred twenty-two thousand, nine hundred two. Explanation: Hayley did not understand that the 9 was in the hundreds place and that the 0 in the tens place meant that there were no tens.

9. 5½ inches; Explanation: The end of the pencil is about halfway between the ruler's five-inch mark and its six-inch mark.

10. rectangular prisms, cubes, and cylinders; Explanation: Rectangular prisms and cubes have flat faces and do not roll. Cylinders could also be used because they have flat faces on opposite sides and can be stacked end to end.

NUMBER AND OPERATIONS

11. Four friends raised money for the Community Cleanup Fund. Study the table. Who was the top fundraiser? Who came in second, third, and fourth? How do you know?

Cleanup Fund	
Child	Amount
Max	$547
Marge	$592
Maury	$447
Mimi	$474

NUMBER AND OPERATIONS

12. The number of books borrowed last year from four libraries are as follows: North City—997,443; South City—897,453; East City—896,453; and West City—997,453. From which library did people borrow the most books? The least books? How do you know?

NUMBER AND OPERATIONS

13. I am a four-digit number. The digit with the greatest place value is 8. The digit with the least place value is 6. The digit in my hundreds place is 3 more than the digit in my tens place and 1 less than the digit in my ones place. What number am I? How do you know?

?,???

ALGEBRA

14. Patty added the last three numbers to the pattern. Are her numbers correct? How do you know?

0, 6, 12, 18, 24, 30, **36, 41, 47**

DATA ANALYSIS AND PROBABILITY

15. Study the picture graph. How many more people like the most popular fruit than the least popular one? Tell how you know.

Favorite Fruits	
Bananas	☺☺☺☺☺
Apples	☺☺☺☺
Grapes	☺☺☺☺☺☺
Pears	☺☺
Key: ☺ = 2 people	

Answer Key

11. first place—Marge, second place—Max, third place—Mimi, fourth place—Maury; Explanation: Compare and order the amounts listed in the table.

12. most—West City, least—East City;
Explanation: Compare and order the numbers.

13. 8,526; Explanation: The 8 is in the thousands place. The 6 is in the ones place. Subtract 1 from 6 to get 5 in the hundreds place. Subtract 3 from 5 to get 2 in the tens place.

14. no; Explanation: The last three numbers should be 36, 42, and 48 because the pattern shows that the numbers increase by 6 each time.

15. 8; Explanation: Subtract the total number of people who prefer pears from the total number of people who prefer grapes (14 − 6 = 8).

NUMBER AND OPERATIONS

16. Evan needs to write this number in expanded notation. Use what you know about place value to tell Evan what to do.

645,379

NUMBER AND OPERATIONS

17. Form all the possible numbers with these five digits that you can that have a 2 in the hundreds place. How many numbers did you make? Explain how you got your answers.

NUMBER AND OPERATIONS

18. Misty is thinking of a number that equals 5,000 when it is rounded to the nearest ten, hundred, and thousand. Write three possible numbers she could be thinking of. Tell how you got your answers.

GEOMETRY

19. Name the solid figure described in the riddle. Then list and describe three real-life examples of it.

I have 6 faces. Not all of my faces are the same size. I have 12 edges. What am I?

MEASUREMENT

20. If a snail moves 1 centimeter a minute, how many minutes will it need to move around the edges of this figure? How do you know?

Answer Key

16. 16. 600,000 + 40,000 + 5,000 + 300 + 70 + 9; Write the value of each number based on where it would be written in a place-value chart.

17. 24 (see the list below); Explanation: A list was made of all the possible combinations.

45,278	54,278	74,258	84,257
45,287	54,287	74,285	84,275
47,258	57,248	75,248	85,247
47,285	57,284	75,284	85,274
48,275	58,247	78,245	87,245
48,257	58,274	78,254	87,254

18. any three of the following: 4,995; 4,996; 4,997; 4,998; 4,999; 5,000; 5,001; 5,002; 5,003; 5,004; Explanation: Guess and check by rounding each number to the nearest 10, 100, and 1,000.

19. rectangular prism; Answers will vary.

20. 16 minutes; Explanation: The perimeter of the figure is 16 centimeters.

NUMBER AND OPERATIONS

21. Patti and Paul are going to the movies. Each will buy a ticket, some popcorn, and a soda. Patti thinks they will each need $12.00 to cover the costs. Paul thinks $10.00 is enough. Whose estimate is more reasonable? Why?

```
           Prices
Movie Ticket    $6.50
Popcorn         $3.25
Soda            $1.50
```

NUMBER AND OPERATIONS

22. Nina chose three different number cards from a stack. Each number is less than 20. No number is odd. The sum of two of the numbers equals the third number. The sum of all three numbers is 24. What number is on each card? Explain how you got your answer.

NUMBER AND OPERATIONS

23. Marcus scored a total of 87 points in two games. On Friday he scored 48 points. On Saturday he scored 39 points. When Marcus added to find his total number of points, did he need to regroup? Why or why not?

ALGEBRA

24. In the first inning of the baseball game, the snack bar workers sold 3 sodas and 2 bags of popcorn. During the second inning, they sold 6 sodas and 4 bags of popcorn. In the third inning, they sold 9 sodas and 6 bags of popcorn. If this pattern continues, how many sodas and bags of popcorn will they sell in the ninth inning? Create a table to continue the pattern.

GEOMETRY

25. Harry painted a figure that has a perimeter of 36 inches. The figure has equal sides that are each 6 inches long. What is the name of the figure? How do you know your answer is correct?

Answer Key

21. Patti's; To get her estimate, Patti rounded the cost of each item to the nearest dollar (Tickets = $7.00; Popcorn = $3.00; Soda = $2.00). The exact amount needed is $11.25. Patti's estimate covers the cost of the items.

22. 4, 8, and 12; Explanation: Guess and check using even numbers less than 20.

23. yes; Since 8 + 9 = 17 and 17 is more than ten ones, ten of the ones must be regrouped to form one ten.

24. 27 sodas and 18 bags of popcorn

Inning	Sodas	Popcorn
1	3	2
2	6	4
3	9	6
4	12	8
5	15	10
6	18	12
7	21	14
8	24	16
9	27	18

25. hexagon; Explanation: Divide 36 by 6. A figure with six sides is a hexagon.

NUMBER AND OPERATIONS

26. Keisha collected 24 seashells at the beach on Monday, 36 seashells on Tuesday, and 48 seashells on Wednesday. On Thursday she sold 50 of the shells she collected to tourists. How many shells does she have left? How do you know?

NUMBER AND OPERATIONS

27. Find the sum of these numbers. Then write a step-by-step explanation telling how you got your answer.

$$\begin{array}{r} 457 \\ + 364 \\ \hline \end{array}$$

NUMBER AND OPERATIONS

28. Solve the number sentence. Then write a story problem to match it.

$$495 + 125 = ?$$

MEASUREMENT

29. Tommy estimates that this eraser is 3 inches long. Is this a reasonable estimate? Tell how you know.

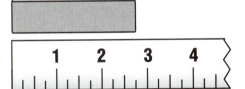

DATA ANALYSIS AND PROBABILITY

30. Study the line plot. Based on its data, about how many raisins should you expect to find in a snack box? How can you tell?

```
                    x
                    x
                  x x
          x x x x x
        x x x x x x
       38 39 40 41 42 43
       Number of Raisins in a Box
```

Answer Key

26. 58 seashells; 24 + 36 + 48 = 108; 108 − 50 = 58

27. 821; Explanation: Answers will vary but should mention regrouping in the ones, tens, and hundreds columns.

28. 620; Story problems will vary but should include words that signal addition such as *total, in all,* or *altogether.*

29. yes; Explanation: The measurement is within ¼ inch of the eraser's actual length.

30. 41; 41 has the most X's on the line plot.

NUMBER AND OPERATIONS

31. The sum of two three-digit addends is 606. The digits in the addends are 1, 2, 3, 4, 5, and 6. What are the addends? How do you know?

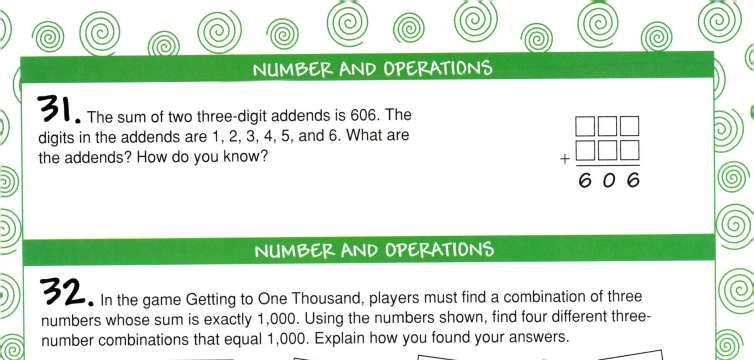

NUMBER AND OPERATIONS

32. In the game Getting to One Thousand, players must find a combination of three numbers whose sum is exactly 1,000. Using the numbers shown, find four different three-number combinations that equal 1,000. Explain how you found your answers.

NUMBER AND OPERATIONS

33. To sell out their first concert, the Music Makers need to sell 5,000 tickets. They have already sold 3,268 tickets. How many more tickets does the band need to sell? Tell how you found out.

DATA ANALYSIS AND PROBABILITY

34. The data Juan collected are in the table. Use the data to construct a line plot.

Classmate Shoe Sizes

Shoe Sizes	Number of Classmates
3	2
4	5
5	8
6	6
7	5

MEASUREMENT

35. Darrell is using paper clips to measure the width of his skateboard. He needs 7 paper clips to measure it. Each paper clip is about 3 centimeters long. How many centimeters wide is the skateboard? Explain how you know.

Answer Key

31. Possible answers include the following: 365 and 241, 245 and 361, 345 and 261; Explanation: Guess and check different number combinations.

32.
- 185 + 500 + 315
- 195 + 500 + 305
- 275 + 500 + 225
- 135 + 365 + 500

Explanation: Guess and check different number combinations.

33. 1,732 tickets; Explanation: Subtract the number of tickets sold (3,268) from the number of tickets needed to sell out the concert (5,000).

34.
```
            x
            x
            x   x
        x   x   x   x
        x   x   x   x
        x   x   x   x
    x   x   x   x   x
    x   x   x   x   x
    3   4   5   6   7
```
Classmate Shoe Sizes

35. 21 centimeters; Explanation: Each paper clip is about 3 centimeters long, and seven paper clips were needed to measure the width: 7 x 3 = 21.

NUMBER AND OPERATIONS

36. Over the weekend Sarah planted 92 flowers, and Liza planted 66 flowers. How many more flowers did Sarah plant than Liza? Explain how you found your answer.

NUMBER AND OPERATIONS

37. During a cookie sale, Stacey sold 28 fewer boxes than Lisa. Lisa sold 35 fewer boxes than Nicole. Nicole sold 49 fewer boxes than Ashley. If Ashley sold 124 boxes of cookies, how many did each of the other girls sell? How do you know?

NUMBER AND OPERATIONS

38. Alex was using 873 blocks. He put 396 back in the container. Alex estimates that he has about 480 blocks left. Do you agree? Why?

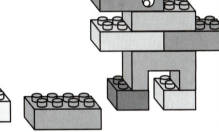

ALGEBRA

39. Elizabeth knows that if 24 + 36 = 60, then 60 − 36 = 24, but she can't explain why. Use a two-digit fact family of your choice to explain how addition and subtraction are related.

$$24 + 36 = 60 \qquad 60 - 36 = 24$$

GEOMETRY

40. Cory drew a polygon that has four sides and no right angles. Only one pair of its sides is parallel. Name and draw this figure.

Answer Key

36. 26; Explanation: Subtract 66 from 92.

37.
- Nicole—75
- Lisa—40
- Stacey—12

Explanation: Work backward.
- To find Nicole's total, subtract 49 from 124 (Ashley's total).
- To find Lisa's total, subtract 35 from 75 (Nicole's total).
- To find Stacey's total, subtract 28 from 40 (Lisa's total).

38. yes; Alex has 477 blocks left, which when rounded to the nearest ten, is 480.

39. Answers will vary but should include that addition and subtraction are inverse operations.

40. trapezoid

NUMBER AND OPERATIONS

41. T. J. collected 567 baseball cards. His friend Lamont collected 399 baseball cards. How many more cards does Lamont need to collect to equal T. J.'s total? How did you get your answer?

NUMBER AND OPERATIONS

42. Describe three different real-life situations that match this number sentence.

$$365 - 55 = 310$$

NUMBER AND OPERATIONS

43. How can you use what you know about addition to check a subtraction problem? Use a sample problem to explain your answer.

DATA ANALYSIS AND PROBABILITY

44. Anna asked 20 people to choose their favorite kind of cookie. Nine people chose chocolate chip. Four chose oatmeal raisin. Three people chose sugar, and four chose peanut butter. Show Anna's data on a bar graph.

MEASUREMENT

45. Mario and Tara measured the length of the school hallway and found that it was 3,000 centimeters. Mario says that this measurement is the same as 3 meters. Tara thinks that it's 30 meters. Who is correct? How do you know?

Answer Key

41. 168; Explanation: Subtract 399 (Lamont's total) from 567 (T. J.'s total).

42. Answers will vary but should match the number sentence.

43. Answers will vary but should show a subtraction problem and an addition problem that use the same numbers, such as 24 − 16 = 8 and 16 + 8 = 24.

44.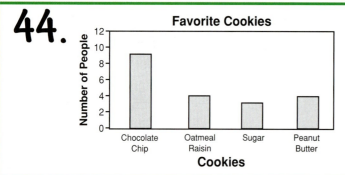

45. Tara; Explanation: There are 100 centimeters in a meter, and 3,000 ÷ 100 = 30.

NUMBER AND OPERATIONS

46. The ice-cream shop has 24 more banana bars for sale than fudge bars. There are 148 banana bars and fudge bars for sale in all. How many are there of each treat? Explain how you got your answer.

NUMBER AND OPERATIONS

47. Today is Dante's grandfather's birthday. He is younger than 60 but older than 40. The sum of the digits of his age is a multiple of six. The digits in his age are not the same, but they are both multiples of four. How old is Dante's grandfather? How did you solve this problem?

NUMBER AND OPERATIONS

48. What is the difference between finding the sum and finding the product of two numbers?

GEOMETRY

49. Megan drew an isosceles triangle. One side measures 12 centimeters. Another side measures 4 centimeters. What are the possible lengths of the third side? How do you know?

ALGEBRA

50. Complete the table using the rule $x - 7 = y$.

x	y
15	__
__	18
22	__
__	25

Answer Key

46. 86 banana bars and 62 fudge bars; Explanation: Guess and check different number combinations whose sum is 148 and whose difference is 24.

47. 48; Explanation: Guess and check different numbers between 40 and 60 to find the one that matches all the clues.

48. Finding the sum means adding. Finding the product means multiplying.

49. 4 centimeters or 12 centimeters; An isosceles triangle has two equal sides.

50.

x	y
15	8
25	18
22	15
32	25

NUMBER AND OPERATIONS

51. Kathryn is planting her garden. She wants to arrange 36 plants in at least two rows. She also wants to have the same number of plants in each row. How many different ways can she arrange the plants? Tell how you know.

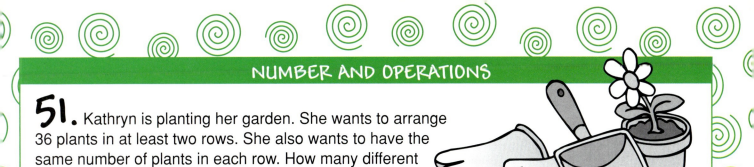

NUMBER AND OPERATIONS

52. There are 25 students in Mike's class. He wants to give each classmate a small bag with 12 pieces of candy inside. Mike thinks he will have enough candy if he buys a bag with at least 200 pieces. Is he right? Explain your answer.

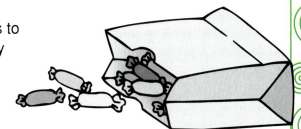

NUMBER AND OPERATIONS

53. Three friends entered a milk-drinking contest. When the contest ended, Lee had six rows of five empty glasses. Mark had four rows of seven empty glasses, and Andre had eight rows of three empty glasses. Who is the winner? How do you know?

DATA ANALYSIS AND PROBABILITY

54. Ms. Cox's class asked people to name their favorite kind of pie. Use the results in the table to make a picture graph. Create a related symbol to represent every two responses.

Favorite Pies

Type of Pie	Number of People
Apple	6
Pumpkin	9
Pecan	10
Coconut	4
Key Lime	7

MEASUREMENT

55. Sharon is buying sugar for her bakery. Each large bag of sugar in her cart weighs one kilogram. Each small bag weighs 500 grams. What is the total weight of the sugar in kilograms? In grams? Tell what you did to find each answer.

Answer Key

51. 7
- 2 rows of 18 plants
- 3 rows of 12 plants
- 4 rows of 9 plants
- 6 rows of 6 plants
- 9 rows of 4 plants
- 12 rows of 3 plants
- 18 rows of 2 plants

52. no; Explanation: The estimate is too low. Mike needs 300 pieces of candy (25 x 12 = 300).

53. Lee; He has the most empty glasses (6 x 5 = 30).

54. Symbols for the picture graph will vary.

Favorite Pies	
Apple	▽▽▽
Pumpkin	▽▽▽▽▼
Pecan	▽▽▽▽
Coconut	▽▽
Key Lime	▽▽▽▼

▽ = 2 people

55. 7 kilograms; 7,000 grams; Explanation: Each large bag equals 1 kilogram or 1,000 grams. Each small bag equals .5 kilograms or 500 grams.

```
3 large bags = 3 kilograms        3 large bags = 3,000 grams
8 small bags = 4 kilograms        8 small bags = 4,000 grams
       total = 7 kilograms               total = 7,000 grams
```

NUMBER AND OPERATIONS

56. Tavon is thinking of an even number. Study the clues to find out what the number is. Then tell how you got your answer.

Clues
- less than 8 x 8
- greater than 7 x 6
- a multiple of 4 and 7

NUMBER AND OPERATIONS

57. Chuck wants to pack 165 pieces of chocolate in 18 boxes. If each box can hold exactly 9 chocolates, does he have enough boxes? How do you know?

NUMBER AND OPERATIONS

58. For the school canned food drive, the third grade collected 427 cans. The second grade collected 653 cans. The fourth grade collected three times as many cans as the third grade. The fifth grade collected six times as many cans as the second grade. How many cans did the second through fifth grades collect all together? Explain how you got your answer.

ALGEBRA

59. Kathy needs to figure out the pattern of these numbers. What is the pattern? List the next five numbers.

27, 32, 30, 35, 33, 38, 36, 41, ___, ___, ___, ___, ___

GEOMETRY

60. In the trapezoid shown, which angles measure more than a right angle? Which angles measure less than a right angle? Tell how you know.

Answer Key

56. 56; Explanation: List the multiples of 4 and 7 that are between 42 and 64. Then identify the common multiple.

57. no; There is only space for 162 pieces of candy in the boxes because 9 x 18 = 162. He needs space for 165 pieces of candy.

58. 6,279 cans; Explanation: To find the total number for the fourth grade, multiply 427 x 3 = 1,281. To find the total for the fifth grade, multiply 653 x 6 = 3,918. Then add the four amounts together to find the total number of cans collected.

59. Add five and then subtract two; 39, 44, 42, 47, 45

60. Angles 1 and 2 measure more than a right angle. Angles 3 and 4 measure less than a right angle. Explanation: A right angle looks like a square corner and measures 90 degrees.

NUMBER AND OPERATIONS

61. David is learning how to multiply two-digit numbers. Help him solve this problem by explaining one step at a time what he should do.

$$\begin{array}{r} 56 \\ \times\ 73 \\ \hline \end{array}$$

NUMBER AND OPERATIONS

62. Shannon knows all of her multiplication facts. How will this help her solve division problems?

NUMBER AND OPERATIONS

63. Study the number sentence. Write a story problem that matches it.

$$36 \div 4 = 9$$

DATA ANALYSIS AND PROBABILITY

64. Ms. Johnson's fourth-grade class created this circle graph. If there are 24 students in her class, how many students have each type of pet? Use data from the graph to support your answers.

Our Pets at Home (cats, dogs, fish, birds)

MEASUREMENT

65. List ten items you would buy at a grocery store. Which items would be weighed in ounces? Which ones would be weighed in pounds? Explain how you know.

Answer Key

61.
1. Multiply 56 by 3 to get 168.
2. Write 0 to hold the ones place and multiply 56 by 7 to show 3,920.
3. Add to get 4,088.

62. Division is the inverse operation of multiplication. By knowing her multiplication facts, she'll be able to answer division problems. Example: 2 x 8 = 16, so 16 ÷ 2 = 8.

63. Answers will vary.

64. Twelve have dogs (½ of 24 = 12).
Six have cats (¼ of 24 = 6).
Three have birds (⅛ of 24 = 3).
Three have fish (⅛ of 24 = 3).

65. Answers will vary.

NUMBER AND OPERATIONS

66. At a birthday party, 72 pieces of candy were evenly divided among 6 friends. Fifty-six pieces of candy were evenly shared among a different group of 4 friends. In which group did each friend end up with more candy? How do you know?

NUMBER AND OPERATIONS

67. A group of 6 friends baked 124 cupcakes to divide evenly among themselves. How many whole cupcakes will each person take home? Explain how you got your answer.

NUMBER AND OPERATIONS

68. Explain one step at a time how you would use base ten blocks to solve this problem.

$$44 \div 6 = ?$$

GEOMETRY

69. Workers at Angle Town Printing Shop charge $0.05 for every acute angle they print, $0.10 for every obtuse angle, and $0.25 for every right angle. Read the word on the sign. How much would this sign cost to print? Tell how you got your answer.

DATA ANALYSIS AND PROBABILITY

70. Ben tracked the daily temperature for a week. He wants to show the data on a graph. Which type of graph is better for showing Ben's data: a bar graph or a line graph? Explain your answer.

Answer Key

66. the group of four friends; The group of four friends each got 14 pieces of candy. The group of six friends only got 12 pieces each.

67. 20; After dividing 124 by 6, there are four cupcakes left over which cannot be divided evenly without cutting them into thirds.

68.
1. Represent 44 with four rods and four cubes.
2. Trade each rod for a group of ten cubes.
3. Form six equal groups of cubes. Two cubes will be left over.

69. Explanation: $2.00 ($0.30 + $0.20 + $1.50)
    6 acute angles ($0.05 x 6 = $0.30)
    2 obtuse angles ($0.10 x 2 = $0.20)
    6 right angles ($0.25 x 6 = $1.50)

70. line graph; Explanation: A line graph shows changes in data over time.

NUMBER AND OPERATIONS

71. Annie wants to divide 58 pretzels among three friends and herself. Can she do this with no pretzels left over? Why or why not?

NUMBER AND OPERATIONS

72. The Wild Animals Club is taking a field trip to the zoo. The 94 club members will ride in vans that can each hold 8 members. How many vans will the club need for the trip? Explain how you got your answer.

NUMBER AND OPERATIONS

73. Patti baked oatmeal cookies and sugar cookies for her birthday party. She placed five cookies in each of six bags and had four cookies left over. If Patti baked 16 oatmeal cookies, how many sugar cookies did she bake? How do you know?

MEASUREMENT

74. Find the temperature on each thermometer. Then write about a real-life situation that matches each temperature.

ALGEBRA

75. Use the digits 7, 8, and 56 to make a fact family. Explain the pattern you see.

Answer Key

71. no, 58 ÷ 4 = 14 R2

72. 12 vans; Explanation: Eleven vans can each carry 8 people for a total of 88 people. A 12th van will be needed to carry the remaining 6 people.

73. 18; Explanation: A total of 34 cookies were baked (5 x 6 = 30, 30 + 4 = 34). To find the number of sugar cookies, subtract 16 (the number of oatmeal cookies) from the total number of cookies baked (34).

74. 40°F, 80°F. Answers will vary.

75. 7 x 8 = 56
8 x 7 = 56
56 ÷ 7 = 8
56 ÷ 8 = 7
Explanation: Multiplication and division are inverse operations. The number sentences in a fact family use the same numbers to show two division problems and two multiplication problems.

NUMBER AND OPERATIONS

76. Steven wants to display his rock collection. When he places his rocks in groups of 2, 4, or 7, there is one rock left over. When he places them in groups of 3 or 9, there are two rocks left over. What is the smallest number of rocks that Steven could have in his collection? How do you know?

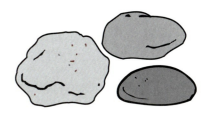

NUMBER AND OPERATIONS

77. Stacey thinks that the quotient of the first problem shown is less than the quotient of the second problem shown. Do you agree? Why or why not?

$$480 \div 6 = ? \qquad 360 \div 4 = ?$$

NUMBER AND OPERATIONS

78. Brad and two friends earned $467 last month washing cars. He needs to divide the money evenly among his partners and himself. Any money left over will be used to buy supplies. How much did each person earn? How much was left over for supplies? Tell how you got your answer.

ALGEBRA

79. Carrie makes cards. When she puts 4 pieces of paper in her card-making machine, 12 cards come out. When she puts 5 pieces of paper in the machine, 15 cards pop out. When she places 6 pieces of paper in the machine, 18 cards come out. If she places 10 pieces of paper in the machine, how many cards will it make? How do you know your answer is correct?

GEOMETRY

80. Your friend Cassie does not know the difference between similar and congruent figures. If she asked you to explain the difference, what would you say? Draw examples to support your answer.

The difference is that...

Answer Key

76. 29; Explanation: Guess and check the numbers that are two more than each multiple of 9 until you find the number that matches all of the clues.

77. yes; The quotient of the first problem is 80, and the quotient of the second problem is 90.

78. $155 per person, $2 for supplies; Explanation: Brad divided $467 by 3, which gave each partner and himself $155. He had $2 left over.

79. 30; Explanation: Multiply 10 by 3 or create an input/output table to continue the pattern.

In	Out
4	12
5	15
6	18
7	21
8	24
9	27
10	30

80. Congruent figures are the same size and the same shape. Similar figures are the same shape but are different sizes. Examples should be drawn.

NUMBER AND OPERATIONS

81. Tommy solved the problem shown and got 164 as his answer. Is it correct? Explain how he can use multiplication to check his answer.

$$985 \div 6 = ?$$

NUMBER AND OPERATIONS

82. Marie says that the quotient of the problem shown will have a 0. Explain how she could know this. Then solve the problem to find the exact answer.

$$3\overline{)325}$$

NUMBER AND OPERATIONS

83. Molly knows that one number is divisible by another number if the quotient is a whole number and the remainder is 0. She must tell whether the number shown is divisible by 3. Is it? How do you know?

ALGEBRA

84. Wade needs to place these bags on a scale so that both sides are balanced. Which bags should he place together? Tell how you know.

 9 lb. 35 lb. 16 lb. 28 lb. 14 lb.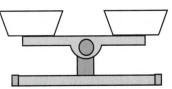

DATA ANALYSIS AND PROBABILITY

85. A ski resort owner surveyed his guests and collected the data shown in the table. Which type of graph should he use to show the data? Why?

Favorite Winter Activities	
Activity	Number of People
Skiing	45
Snowboarding	60
Snowshoeing	50
Tubing	75

Answer Key

81. no; The correct answer is 164 R1. To check a division problem, multiply the quotient by the divisor. Then add the remainder. If the answer is equal to the dividend, the problem is correct.

82. There is a 2 in the tens place, and 2 cannot be divided by 3. The exact answer is 108 R1.

83. yes; Explanation: When 534 is divided by 3, there is no remainder. Or use a divisibility rule: A number is divisible by 3 if the sum of its digits (12) is divisible by 3.

84. Put the bags weighing 28 pounds, 14 pounds, and 9 pounds together on one side and the bags weighing 35 pounds and 16 pounds together on the other side. This makes the bags grouped on each side of the scale have the same total weight (51 pounds).

85. either a bar graph or a picture graph; These types of graphs are used to compare data.

NUMBER AND OPERATIONS

86. Todd wants to find the average of these numbers. List the steps he should follow to find the answer.

56   65   58   61   75

NUMBER AND OPERATIONS

87. The answer to Jamie's riddle is 177. First, he subtracted 16 from his starting number. Then he added 25. Next, he multiplied by 3. What number did Jamie start with? How do you know?

NUMBER AND OPERATIONS

88. Megan and Sarah earned $156 at their lemonade stand last week and divided the money evenly. This week, Megan worked alone. She sold brownies and earned three times as much as she did selling lemonade. How much did Megan earn in all for both weeks? Tell how you got your answer.

MEASUREMENT

89. Do these clocks both show the same time? Explain how you know.

GEOMETRY

90. Study the figures. Which ones are congruent? Which are similar? How can you tell?

Answer Key

86. Add all five numbers together; then divide the total by 5. The mean is 63.

87. 50; Explanation: Work backward, using inverse operations and the following steps to find the starting number.
1. Divide 177 by 3 to get 59.
2. Subtract 25 from 59 to get 34.
3. Add 16 to 34 to get 50.

88. $312; Explanation: Use three different operations to find the answer.
1. Divide $156 by 2 to get $78.
2. Multiply $78 by 3 to get $234.
3. Add $78 to $234 to get $312.

89. no; Explanation: The digital clock shows 6:50. The regular clock shows 4:50.

90. A and D are congruent, and B and C are similar; Explanation: A and D are congruent because they are the same size and shape. B and C are similar because they are the same shape but are different sizes.

NUMBER AND OPERATIONS

91. Ty wants to buy a $3.95 comic book with the money he's saved. Does he have enough? Tell how you got your answer.

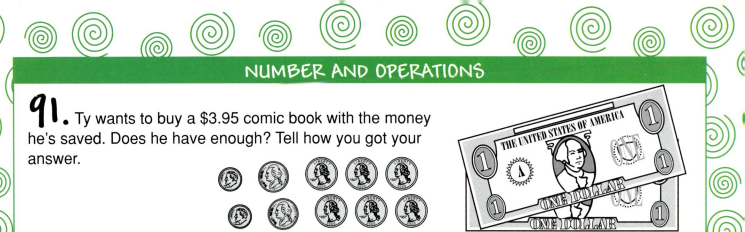

NUMBER AND OPERATIONS

92. Brad has $0.79 in his pocket. He has at least one penny, one nickel, one dime, and one quarter. He has no silver dollars or 50-cent pieces. How many different combinations of coins could he have in his pocket? Explain how you know.

NUMBER AND OPERATIONS

93. Sara's grandfather buys a regular cup of coffee every day for $0.50 except on Sunday when he gets a flavored cup for $1.20. What is the total amount he will spend for the first 15 days of March? How do you know your answer is correct?

ALGEBRA

94. Shawna needs help multiplying this problem. Tell her how to use the distributive property to find the answer.

387 x 5 = ?

GEOMETRY

95. Bobby used cutouts of capital letters to spell his name in a vertical line. Then he flipped each letter to the right. When he did this, some letters looked the same and some looked different. Why?

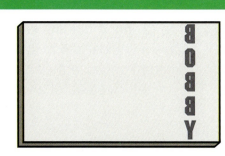

Answer Key

91. no; Explanation: He only has $3.80. He needs $0.15 more.

92. 24; Explanation: Make an organized list.

Q	D	N	P
2	2	1	4
2	1	3	4
2	1	2	9
2	1	1	14
1	4	2	4
1	4	1	9
1	3	3	9
1	3	4	4

Q	D	N	P
1	3	2	14
1	3	1	19
1	3	2	14
1	3	1	19
1	2	5	9
1	2	6	4
1	2	4	14
1	2	3	19

Q	D	N	P
1	2	2	24
1	1	8	4
1	1	7	9
1	1	6	14
1	1	5	19
1	1	4	24
1	1	3	29
1	1	2	34
1	1	1	39

93. $8.90; He'll buy regular coffee on 13 days ($0.50 x 13 = $6.50) and flavored coffee on two days ($1.20 x 2 = $2.40) for a total of $8.90 ($6.50 + $2.40 = $8.90).

94. (300 x 5) + (80 x 5) + (7 x 5) = 1,500 + 400 + 35 = 1,935

95. The *O* and *Y* look the same because they each have a vertical line of symmetry. The *B*s look different because they have a horizontal line of symmetry instead of a vertical line of symmetry.

NUMBER AND OPERATIONS

96. Snow cones, sundaes, flavored pops, and ice-cream sandwiches are being sold at the school carnival. The prices are $2.25, $1.50, $1.85, and $1.20. Use the clues to match each treat with its price. Explain how you got your answers.
- Ice-cream sandwiches cost more than flavored pops.
- Sundaes cost the most.
- Neither the flavored pops nor the snow cones cost $1.50.

NUMBER AND OPERATIONS

97. Barry has saved three $5 bills, two $1 bills, 2 quarters, 5 dimes, and 3 pennies. Gary has saved two $5 bills, six $1 bills, 3 quarters, 8 dimes, 6 nickels, and 8 pennies. Who has saved more? How do you know?

NUMBER AND OPERATIONS

98. Ian's mom stopped at a store to buy food for his grandmother's birthday dinner. About how much money will she need to pay the bill? Explain why your answer is reasonable.

Corner Market
$5.99
$3.25
$12.56
$2.18

MEASUREMENT

99. Three friends are comparing their work schedules for March at the sandwich shop. Tim will work every second day. Tom will work every third day. Todd will work every fourth day. How many times will all three friends be working on the same dates? Tell how you got your answer.

DATA ANALYSIS AND PROBABILITY

100. Tyler is holding five number cards. If the range of the numbers is 88, what number is on the fifth card? How do you know?

Answer Key

96.
sundaes—$2.25
snow cones—$1.85
ice-cream sandwiches—$1.50
flavored pops—$1.20

97. Barry; He saved $18.03. Gary only saved $17.93.

98. about $24; Explanation: Round each amount to the nearest dollar and add.

99. twice—on March 12 and March 24; Explanation: Find the common multiples of 2, 3, and 4, or make a table.

100. 22 or 123; The range is the difference between the largest and smallest numbers.

NUMBER AND OPERATIONS

101. Erin's mom is taking her to Rhonda's Restaurant for the breakfast buffet. They arrive at 7:30 A.M. How much will their meal cost? Explain how you got your answer.

Rhonda's Restaurant
Adults $5.50
Children $3.00
Discount Before 8 A.M. $1.50 per person

NUMBER AND OPERATIONS

102. Josh has $10.00 to spend on three items he will give to an outdoor play center. Which two combinations of items can he buy to spend exactly $10.00? Explain your choices.

scoop ball set—$2.25
plastic hoop—$6.00
kickball—$6.25
bubbles—$1.75
jump rope—$1.50

NUMBER AND OPERATIONS

103. Stella and her mom went grocery shopping. The bill was $75.28. Her mom gave the cashier $100.00. Stella thinks her mom will get $24.82 in change. Is she correct? Why or why not?

ALGEBRA

104. Use this rule to find the possible values of y when x equals 3, 6, 9, 12, or 15. Construct a table to show your answers.

$$y = 6x$$

GEOMETRY

105. Katie is thinking about different kinds of lines. Name a capital letter that could represent each type of line. Tell why you chose each letter.

Intersecting? Perpendicular? Parallel?

Answer Key

101. $5.50; Explanation:

$5.50	$3.00	$4.00
− 1.50	− 1.50	+ 1.50
$4.00	$1.50	$5.50

102. scoop ball set, bubbles, and plastic hoop
kickball, scoop ball set, and jump rope

103. no; Her mom will get $24.72 in change instead of $24.82.

104.

x	y
3	18
6	36
9	54
12	72
15	90

105. Answers for perpendicular and parallel lines will vary. Possible answers include the following.
- X—intersecting (has segments that cross at one point)
- T—perpendicular (has segments that form right angles)
- H—parallel (has segments that are the same distance apart and never cross)

NUMBER AND OPERATIONS

106. Paula created this problem. Solve it; then write a story problem that matches it.

$$\$85.00 - \$42.50 = ?$$

NUMBER AND OPERATIONS

107. A birthday buffet at Peppi's Pizza Palace costs $5.45 per guest, but the birthday kid is free. If Nate invited 12 friends to his party, what would the cost be? Explain how you know.

NUMBER AND OPERATIONS

108. Paula's afterschool popcorn business made $190.80 in profits last month. She gets to keep half of the profits. Then she divides the rest equally among her five workers. How much will each worker get? Tell how you got your answer.

MEASUREMENT

109. Dave's Dog Grooming Shop has a lot of one-hour appointments on its schedule today. Use the clues to find out when each dog will be groomed. Tell how you know your answers are correct.

- Max goes 5 hours before Molly.
- Murray goes 1 hour after Max but 1 hour before Millie.
- Millie goes at 11:00 A.M.
- Muggs goes 3 hours after Murray.

DATA ANALYSIS AND PROBABILITY

110. Each day last week Matt solved a certain number of story problems for a math contest. Then he found the mean, median, mode, and range of his data. He thinks the mean is 11, the median is 14, the mode is 8, and the range is 4. Are his answers correct? How do you know?

Day	Number of Problems
Monday	8
Tuesday	13
Wednesday	14
Thursday	8
Friday	12

Answer Key

106. $42.50; Stories will vary but should match the number sentence.

107. $65.40; Explanation: 12 x $5.45 = $65.40

108. $19.08; Explanation: $190.80 ÷ 2 = $95.40, $95.40 ÷ 5 = $19.08

109.
- Max—9:00 A.M.
- Murray—10:00 A.M.
- Millie—11:00 A.M.
- Muggs—1:00 P.M.
- Molly—2:00 P.M.

110. no; Two are wrong: The median should be 12 and the range should be 6. Explanation: To find the median, arrange the numbers from least to greatest; the number in the middle is the median. To find the range, subtract the smallest number from the largest number. To find the mean, divide the sum of the number of problems by five. The mode is the most repeated number.

NUMBER AND OPERATIONS

111. David wants to buy 15 oranges. How much will he have to pay at this price? Tell how you got your answer.

6 for $1.08

NUMBER AND OPERATIONS

112. Brent is buying balloons for a party. At Party Place he can buy ten balloons for $4.00. At Celebration City he can buy three for $1.50 and get one free. At which store will he get the better deal? How do you know?

NUMBER AND OPERATIONS

113. A cake at Barb's Bakery was cut into 12 pieces. Eight pieces were sold. What fraction of the cake was not sold? Explain how you got your answer.

ALGEBRA

114. Study the boxes. Based on this pattern, how many sections will each of the next three boxes have? Tell how you know your answers are correct.

Box 1   Box 2   Box 3

GEOMETRY

115. Study the drawings. Use them to explain what a polygon is. Tell why your answer is correct.

These are polygons.

These are not polygons.

Answer Key

111. $2.70; Explanation: Divide $1.08 by 6 to get $0.18 (the price of one orange). Then multiply $0.18 by 15 to get $2.70.

112. Celebration City; Explanation: Balloons at Celebration City cost about $0.38 each compared to $0.40 each at Party Place.

113. $4/12$ or $1/3$

114. 20, 30, 42; Explanation: The length and width of each box increases by one row so that the next three boxes will measure 4 x 5, 5 x 6, and 6 x 7.

115. Answers will vary but should show an understanding that a polygon is a closed figure constructed of line segments that do not intersect.

NUMBER AND OPERATIONS

116. Write a fraction that shows the number of vowels in this word. Then write a fraction that shows its number of consonants. Tell how you know your answers are correct.

mathematics

NUMBER AND OPERATIONS

117. Joseph planted $\frac{5}{12}$ of his garden with carrots, $\frac{4}{12}$ with tomatoes, and $\frac{3}{12}$ with peppers. Does this chart represent his garden? Why or why not?

C	C	P
C	T	P
C	T	P
C	T	P

C = Carrots
T = Tomatoes
P = Peppers

NUMBER AND OPERATIONS

118. Jen will use 20 glass beads to make a necklace. Four beads are blue, three are green, five are yellow, and the rest are red. What fraction tells the number of red beads she has? Explain how you know.

MEASUREMENT

119. Julie's mom will volunteer at the school carnival from 10:15 A.M. until 3:05 P.M. Emily's mom will volunteer from 9:35 A.M. until 2:15 P.M. Whose mom will volunteer more time? How much more time? Explain what you did to find the answer.

DATA ANALYSIS AND PROBABILITY

120. Identify the coordinates for each point on this grid. Then tell how you got your answers.

Answer Key

116. vowels—4/11, consonants—7/11

117. no; Explanation: The drawing shows 3/12 tomatoes instead of 4/12, and 4/12 peppers instead of 3/12.

118. 8/20 or 2/5

119. Julie's mom, ten minutes; Explanation: Julie's mom will volunteer for four hours 50 minutes. Emily's mom will volunteer for four hours 40 minutes.

120. A = (2, 2)
B = (3, 4)
C = (4, 1)
D = (1, 3)
Explanation: The first number in the ordered pair tells how far right to move. The second number tells how far up to move.

NUMBER AND OPERATIONS

121. Liz needs three equivalent fractions for $\frac{3}{4}$. Tell her how to find the fractions.

$$\frac{3}{4} = \underline{}, \underline{}, \text{ and } \underline{}$$

NUMBER AND OPERATIONS

122. Trevor and Dillon each poured a glass of soda. Trevor filled his glass $\frac{8}{10}$ full. Dillon filled his glass $\frac{4}{5}$ full. Did they each fill their glasses with the same amount of soda? How do you know?

NUMBER AND OPERATIONS

123. Chuck challenged his friend Matt to write this fraction in simplest form using only one step. By which digit should Matt divide the fraction's numerator and denominator? Explain to Matt why this is the correct digit to use.

$$\frac{12}{18}$$

ALGEBRA

124. Annie and Andre sold doughnuts and donated the money to the animal shelter. Annie sold five times as many doughnuts as Andre. If x represents Andre's total, which expression represents Annie's? Tell how you got your answer.

$5 + x$

$5x$

GEOMETRY

125. Mr. Roberts drew this polygon on the board. He says its sides are all the same length. Scott thinks the figure is a rhombus. Abby thinks it's a square. Who's right? Explain how you know.

Answer Key

121. Answers will vary. To find equivalent fractions, Liz can multiply the numerator and denominator by the same number. Possible answers include $^6/_8$, $^9/_{12}$, and $^{12}/_{16}$.

122. yes; The two fractions are equivalent.

123. 6; Explanation: Six is the greatest common factor of 12 and 18.

124. $5x$; Explanation: $5 + x$ means you add five to whatever number x represents. $5x$ means you multiply five times whatever number x represents, which is what you need to do to discover how many doughnuts Annie sold.

125. Both students are correct; Explanation: A square is a rectangle with congruent sides. A rhombus is a parallelogram with congruent sides.

NUMBER AND OPERATIONS

126. In Emma's class, $\frac{5}{6}$ of the students bring their lunches from home. In Eddie's class, $\frac{4}{5}$ of the students bring their lunches. If each class has 30 students, which class has more students bringing lunches from home? How do you know?

NUMBER AND OPERATIONS

127. Donte lined up two of his miniature cars at one end of his kitchen table. He gave each car a push and measured how far each car traveled. The red car went $\frac{3}{4}$ meter. The blue one went $\frac{5}{8}$ meter. Which car traveled farther? Tell what you did to find the answer.

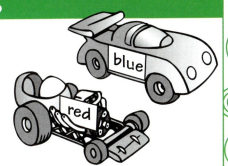

NUMBER AND OPERATIONS

128. Jake needs to sort these fractions into three groups: less than $\frac{1}{2}$, equal to $\frac{1}{2}$, and greater than $\frac{1}{2}$. Explain how he should do this.

$\frac{4}{5}$ $\frac{3}{8}$ $\frac{5}{10}$ $\frac{2}{12}$ $\frac{5}{6}$ $\frac{9}{15}$ $\frac{4}{9}$ $\frac{3}{6}$ $\frac{2}{4}$

MEASUREMENT

129. Penny is making a petal rope to decorate the edge of the table for her aunt's birthday party. If the table measures 8 feet by 4 feet, how long will the rope need to be? How do you know?

DATA ANALYSIS AND PROBABILITY

130. Tell whether you think each event is *certain*, *likely*, or *unlikely* to happen. Explain why you chose each answer.

- The principal will ride a scooter around the school today.
- You will have homework this week.
- The sun will rise tomorrow.

Answer Key

126. Emma's; Explanation: $\frac{5}{6}$ of 30 = 25 and $\frac{4}{5}$ of 30 = 24

127. the red car; One possible way to find the answer would be to draw a picture of each distance. Then compare the two pictures and you'll discover that $\frac{3}{4}$ is more than $\frac{5}{8}$.

128. less than $\frac{1}{2}$—$\frac{3}{8}$, $\frac{2}{12}$, $\frac{4}{9}$
equal to $\frac{1}{2}$—$\frac{5}{10}$, $\frac{3}{6}$, $\frac{2}{4}$
greater than $\frac{1}{2}$—$\frac{4}{5}$, $\frac{5}{6}$, $\frac{9}{15}$

129. 24 feet; Explanation: 8 + 8 + 4 + 4 = 24, or (2 x 8) + (2 x 4) = 24

130. It is *unlikely* that the principal will ride a scooter around the school today.
It is *likely* that you will have homework this week.
It is *certain* that the sun will rise tomorrow.

NUMBER AND OPERATIONS

131. Each pizza at Mindy's party was cut into 8 slices. If Mindy's guests ate a total of 19 pieces of pizza, how much pizza was eaten? Tell how you got your answer.

NUMBER AND OPERATIONS

132. Katie needs $3\frac{2}{3}$ cups of sugar to make taffy. She only has a $\frac{1}{3}$-cup measuring cup. How many times will she have to fill this cup with sugar to get the amount she needs? How do you know?

NUMBER AND OPERATIONS

133. If the buckets used are the same size, would you rather have $\frac{18}{10}$ buckets of quarters or $2\frac{4}{10}$ buckets of quarters? Why?

ALGEBRA

134. Study the problem. Josh thinks that the value of x is 15. Do you agree? Why or why not?

$$3x = 18$$

GEOMETRY

135. Write a riddle about this polygon. Include clues about the number of sides and the number of angles.

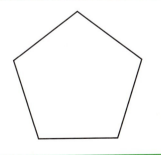

Answer Key

131. $2\frac{3}{8}$ pizzas; One possible way to find the answer would be to draw a picture. The illustration shows that two full pizzas were eaten and $\frac{3}{8}$ of a third pizza were eaten.

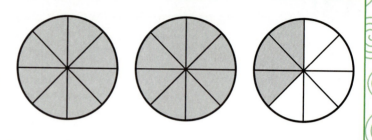

132. 11; Explanation: Three $\frac{1}{3}$ cups equal 1 whole cup. So nine $\frac{1}{3}$ cups would equal 3 cups and two more $\frac{1}{3}$ cups would equal $\frac{2}{3}$ cups. Nine $\frac{1}{3}$ cups + two $\frac{1}{3}$ cups = eleven $\frac{1}{3}$ cups.

133. $2\frac{4}{10}$ buckets; Explanation: $\frac{18}{10} = 1\frac{8}{10}$ or $1\frac{4}{5}$ buckets, which is less than $2\frac{4}{10}$.

134. no; It should be 6 because 3 x 15 is 45, not 18.

135. Answers will vary but should include that the pentagon is a polygon with five sides and five angles.

NUMBER AND OPERATIONS

136. Kara walked $\frac{4}{10}$ mile to the post office. Then she walked another $\frac{2}{10}$ mile to her friend's house. How far did she walk in all? Explain how you got your answer.

NUMBER AND OPERATIONS

137. Ben's basketball team practiced $3\frac{2}{3}$ hours this week. Jimmy's team practiced $2\frac{2}{3}$ hours. How many hours did the brothers practice all together? How do you know?

NUMBER AND OPERATIONS

138. Darrin thinks the answer to this problem is $\frac{6}{16}$. Is he correct? Why or why not?

$$\frac{5}{8} + \frac{1}{8} = ?$$

MEASUREMENT

139. Derek's dad shaded this grid to show the size of the deck he is building for their house. How much wood will it take to cover the shaded area? Tell how you know.

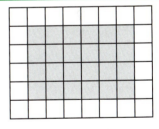

1 unit = 2 ft.

DATA ANALYSIS AND PROBABILITY

140. Each side of Jan's number cube shows a different even number from 1 to 12. If she rolls the cube, what are all the possible outcomes? Tell how you got your answer.

Answer Key

136. $6/10$ mile, or $3/5$ mile; Explanation: $4/10 + 2/10 = 6/10$ or $3/5$.

137. $6\frac{1}{3}$ hours; Explanation: $3\frac{2}{3} + 2\frac{2}{3} = 6\frac{1}{3}$.

138. no, because the answer is $6/8$ or $3/4$; Explanation: When adding like fractions, the denominator remains the same and only the numerators are added.

139. 48 (24 x 2) square feet

140. 2, 4, 6, 8, 10, and 12

NUMBER AND OPERATIONS

141. Jesse's mom bought 5 cases of soda for the soccer team's party. At the end of the party, there were $1\frac{4}{12}$ cases left. How many cases were used? Tell how you know.

NUMBER AND OPERATIONS

142. Rob and Stan each built model ships. Rob's ship is $1\frac{3}{4}$ feet long. Stan's is $1\frac{1}{4}$ foot long. If they put the ships next to each other in a line, how long will they be together?

NUMBER AND OPERATIONS

143. In a group of 10 students, $\frac{3}{10}$ turned in their candy orders on Tuesday, and $\frac{2}{10}$ turned in their candy orders on Wednesday. The rest of the group turned in their orders on Thursday. What fraction of the group turned in their orders on Thursday? How do you know?

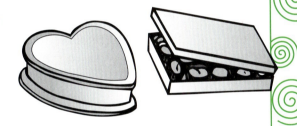

ALGEBRA

144. Before taking lessons, Karen knew 5 different dance steps. After the lessons, she knew a total of 15 dance steps. Write and solve an equation that shows how many new steps Karen learned by taking lessons. Tell how you got your answer.

GEOMETRY

145. Put each polygon in one or more categories. Then explain why you sorted the shapes as you did.

- opposite sides equal in length and parallel
- only one pair of parallel sides
- at least two angles less than 90°

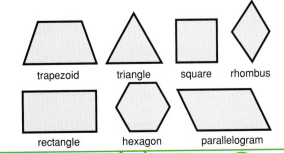

Answer Key

141. $3\frac{8}{12}$, or $3\frac{2}{3}$; One possible way to solve the problem would be to reduce $1\frac{4}{12}$ to $1\frac{1}{3}$, draw a picture of the five cases, and then shade the amount left to reveal the amount used.

142. 3 ft.; $1\frac{3}{4} + 1\frac{1}{4} = 2\frac{4}{4}$ or 3

143. $\frac{5}{10}$ or $\frac{1}{2}$; Explanation: $\frac{3}{10} + \frac{2}{10} = \frac{5}{10}$ or $\frac{1}{2}$. So, if $\frac{1}{2}$ turned in their orders on Tuesday and Wednesday, then $\frac{1}{2}$ turned in their orders on Thursday.

144. $15 - 5 = x$, or $5 + x = 15$; $x = 10$

145.
- opposite sides equal in length and parallel—square, rhombus, parallelogram, rectangle, hexagon
- only one pair of parallel sides—trapezoid
- at least two angles less than 90°—trapezoid, triangle, rhombus, parallelogram

NUMBER AND OPERATIONS

146. Becca ran $1\frac{1}{4}$ mile in the morning and $1\frac{2}{4}$ mile in the evening. How far did she run in all? Did she run farther in the morning or in the evening? How do you know?

NUMBER AND OPERATIONS

147. Four friends joined a bicycle club. Last week they rode $10\frac{1}{4}$ miles. This week they rode $12\frac{3}{4}$ miles. How many miles have they biked so far? Tell what you did to get the answer.

NUMBER AND OPERATIONS

148. Wendy doesn't understand how learning about fractions will help her in real life. Explain three ways fractions are used every day so she'll know how important they are.

$\frac{5}{8}$ a third $\frac{2}{3}$

$\frac{1}{2}$ an eighth $\frac{1}{4}$

MEASUREMENT

149. Eric gets area and perimeter mixed up. Think of an example you could use to help him remember the difference. Explain it using words, numbers, and pictures.

The difference between finding area and perimeter is...

DATA ANALYSIS AND PROBABILITY

150. Of the 20 students in Ms. Murphy's math class, 8 like chocolate ice cream, 7 like vanilla, and 5 like strawberry. What is the probability of one of her students choosing a chocolate ice-cream cone? Vanilla? Strawberry? Explain how you know.

Answer Key

146. $2\frac{3}{4}$, evening; Explanation: $1\frac{1}{4} + 1\frac{2}{4} = 2\frac{3}{4}$; $1\frac{2}{4} = 1\frac{1}{2}$, which is larger than $1\frac{1}{4}$.

147. 23 miles; $10\frac{1}{4} + 12\frac{3}{4} = 22\frac{4}{4}$; $\frac{4}{4} = 1$, so $22\frac{4}{4} = 23$.

148. Answers will vary but should include three different examples.

149. Answers will vary, but should convey that to find the *perimeter* the length of each side is added and to find the *area*, the length and width of the figure are multiplied.

150. chocolate—$\frac{8}{20}$, or $\frac{2}{5}$
vanilla—$\frac{7}{20}$
strawberry—$\frac{5}{20}$, or $\frac{1}{4}$

NUMBER AND OPERATIONS

151. Jeff has 10 soccer balls. Seven of the balls are red. The rest of the balls are white. Write the decimal that shows how many white balls. Tell how you got your answer.

NUMBER AND OPERATIONS

152. Ben doesn't understand why this decimal and fraction represent the same amount. Use a drawing to help him see that one form is equivalent to the other.

$\frac{1}{2}$ 0.5

NUMBER AND OPERATIONS

153. Nikki has 4.2 pounds of clay. Cheri has 4.20 pounds of clay. Cheri thinks she has more clay than Nikki. Is she right? Why or why not?

ALGEBRA

154. Lee hit 15 more home runs than last year's record. Luke hit twice as many home runs as last year's record and more home runs than Lee. Write an expression that shows that Luke hit more home runs than Lee. Explain how you got your answer.

GEOMETRY

155. Tonya needs help figuring out how many lines of symmetry a square has. Use a drawing to explain how she can find the answer.

Answer Key

151. 0.3; Explanation: One possible way to get the answer is to draw a picture. Shade in the seven strips to represent the seven red balls. The remaining three strips represent the white balls.

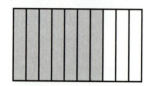

152. Drawings will vary. A possible drawing is shown.

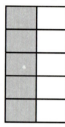

153. no; Both girls have the same amount because 4.2 is the same as 4.20.

154. $x + 15 < 2x$

155. See the figure. A square has 4 lines of symmetry.

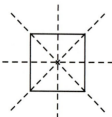

NUMBER AND OPERATIONS

156. Melissa needs at least 8.5 pounds of hamburger meat for a cookout. The butcher gave her 8.25 pounds. Did he give her enough hamburger meat? Tell how you know.

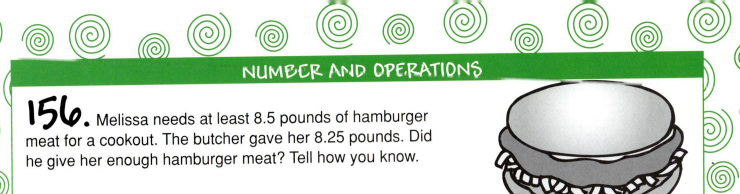

NUMBER AND OPERATIONS

157. Yesterday the track coach timed his sprinters in the order in which they ran. Now he wants to list the times in order from slowest to fastest. Show him how the list should be written.

9.82   9.07
9.7
8.49   8.53

NUMBER AND OPERATIONS

158. Which of these decimals round to the same whole number? Explain how you know.

2.37   1.98   ?
2.51   ?   1.49
?   2.01   1.62   ?

MEASUREMENT

159. Carrie wants new wall-to-wall carpet. If the room measures 11 feet x 15 feet, how much carpet will she need? Tell how you got your answer.

DATA ANALYSIS AND PROBABILITY

160. At Sam's Sandwich Shop, customers can choose between sliced bread or a roll, ham or turkey, and mayonnaise or mustard. How many possible sandwich combinations are there using only one item from each category? Make an organized list to find the answer. Then explain how you made your list.

Answer Key

156. no; Explanation: 8.25 pounds is less than 8.5 pounds. She needs 0.25 pounds more.

157.
9.82—slowest
9.7
9.07
8.53
8.49—fastest

158. The following decimals all round to 2.
2.37, 1.98, 2.01, 1.62

159. 165 square feet; Explanation: to determine the amount of carpet needed, multiply the length by the width. 11 ft. x 15 ft. = 165 square ft.

160. 8 possible combinations:
- sliced bread, ham, mayonnaise
- sliced bread, ham, mustard
- sliced bread, turkey, mayonnaise
- sliced bread, turkey, mustard
- roll, ham, mayonnaise
- roll, ham, mustard
- roll, turkey, mayonnaise
- roll, turkey, mustard

NUMBER AND OPERATIONS

161. Ned solved this problem and got 0.12 as his answer. He doesn't understand why his answer is not correct. Explain to Ned how to get the correct answer.

$$0.6 + 0.06$$

NUMBER AND OPERATIONS

162. Rene hiked 3.85 miles yesterday. Today she hiked 2.9 miles. How many more miles did she hike yesterday than today? How do you know?

NUMBER AND OPERATIONS

163. Gus's Gas Station charges $6.15 for every 3 gallons of gas. How much will it cost a customer to fill a 15-gallon tank? How do you know your answer is correct?

ALGEBRA

164. Liz ordered 3 boxes of flowers to plant in her yard. She got a total of 21 plants. If each box has the same number of plants, how many plants were in each box? Write an equation to solve the problem. Explain how you got your answer.

GEOMETRY

165. Jerry studied this table and is certain that the diameter and radius of a circle are related. Is he correct? Why or why not?

Circle	Radius	Diameter
1	4	8
2	2.5	5
3	5	10

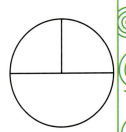

Answer Key

161. The correct answer is 0.66. Ned did not align the decimal points or understand that he was actually adding six hundredths to six tenths.

162. 0.95 mile; Explanation: 3.85 − 2.9 = 0.95

163. $30.75; Explanation: 15 ÷ 3 = 5; 5 × $6.15 = $30.75

164. 21 ÷ 3 = x, or $3x = 21$; $x = 7$

165. yes; The radius is half the diameter. Or the diameter is twice the radius.

NUMBER AND OPERATIONS

166. Eddie can jump three times as far as his younger brother Derek. If Derek can jump 1.57 meters, how far can Eddie jump? How do you know?

NUMBER AND OPERATIONS

167. Study this number line. Where would each of the following fractions be placed on the line: $\frac{3}{4}, \frac{1}{4}, \frac{1}{2}$? Tell why each fraction should be where you placed it.

0   0.25   0.5   0.75   1

NUMBER AND OPERATIONS

168. Cliff has done $\frac{3}{10}$ of his homework. What decimal represents this fraction? What percent? Explain how you know.

MEASUREMENT

169. Sidney is designing a quadrilateral that has a perimeter of 16 units and an area of 15 square units. Draw a picture of what her design would look like. Tell how you know it matches her dimensions.

DATA ANALYSIS AND PROBABILITY

170. Mark studied this spinner. He thinks the probability of spinning a triangle or a square is $\frac{2}{3}$. Is he right? Why or why not?

Answer Key

166. 4.71 meters; Explanation: 1.57 x 3 = 4.71

167.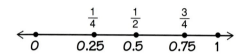

168. 0.3, 30%

169. The picture should show a rectangle that measures either 3 x 5 units or 5 x 3 units.

170. yes; because the triangle and the square are ⅔ of the spinner.

NUMBER AND OPERATIONS

171. Chip says he used the decimal equivalent for $\frac{1}{4}$ to help him find the decimal equivalent for $\frac{3}{4}$. What was his answer? How do you know it is correct?

$\frac{1}{4} = 0.25$

$\frac{3}{4} = ?$

NUMBER AND OPERATIONS

172. How is $\frac{1}{2}$ related to 50% and 0.5? Explain your thinking.

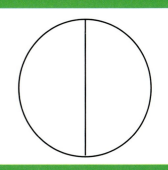

NUMBER AND OPERATIONS

173. Clint said he'd rather be paid $\frac{4}{5}$ of a dollar than 75% of a dollar. Has Clint made a good decision? Explain why or why not.

ALGEBRA

174. Study the equation. The value of the triangle is 3. If the value of each square and circle is greater than 3 but less than 10, what are the possible values of each square and circle? How do you know?

■ + ■ + ■ + ▲ = ● + ● + ●

GEOMETRY

175. Jim used 30 sugar cubes to win a sugar cube–building contest. Could this be Jim's design? Why or why not?

Answer Key

171. 0.75; Multiply 0.25 by 3.

172. All three forms represent the same amount. They are all half of a whole.
- ½ + ½ = 1
- 50% + 50% = 100%
- 0.5 + 0.5 = 1

173. yes; because ⅘ = ⁸⁄₁₀, or 80%, which is more than 75%

174. five possible values for each:
- square = 4, circle = 5
- square = 5, circle = 6
- square = 6, circle = 7
- square = 7, circle = 8
- square = 8, circle = 9

175. yes; (4 rows x 3 cubes each) + (3 rows x 3 cubes each) + (2 rows x 3 cubes each) + (1 row x 3 cubes) = 12 + 9 + 6 + 3 = 30

NUMBER AND OPERATIONS

176. Kim is awake 16 hours a day. If she spends 8 hours in school, what percent of her time awake is she in school? How do you know?

NUMBER AND OPERATIONS

177. Sandy's mom asked her to plant 50% of the 20 flower bulbs she bought. If she plants only 4 bulbs, will that be the correct amount? Why or why not?

NUMBER AND OPERATIONS

178. Joel has $\frac{1}{4}$ of a pound of jelly beans. Jasmine has 0.5 of a pound of jelly beans. Who has the most? Tell how you know.

MEASUREMENT

179. Mr. Peterson wants to cover the floor of his game room with 1' x 1' tiles. Study his floor plan. Based on this drawing, how many pieces of tile will he need? Explain how you got your answer.

DATA ANALYSIS AND PROBABILITY

180. Study the spinners shown that two players will use to play a game. To win a point, Player A will try to spin two numbers that have an odd sum. Player B will try to spin two numbers that have an even sum. Is this game fair? Explain how you know.

Answer Key

176. 50%; because 8 is 50% of 16.

177. no; She should plant 10 bulbs.

178. Jasmine has the most; Explanation: $0.5 = \frac{5}{10}$ or $\frac{1}{2}$; $\frac{1}{2}$ pound is more than $\frac{1}{4}$ pound.

179. 192 square feet

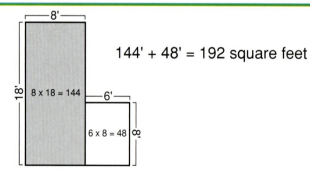

144' + 48' = 192 square feet

180. yes; Explanation: Out of the 16 possible spins, eight produce even sums and eight produce odd sums.

1 + 1 = 2 (even)	2 + 1 = 3 (odd)	3 + 1 = 4 (even)	4 + 1 = 5 (odd)
1 + 2 = 3 (odd)	2 + 2 = 4 (even)	3 + 2 = 5 (odd)	4 + 2 = 6 (even)
1 + 3 = 4 (even)	2 + 3 = 5 (odd)	3 + 3 = 6 (even)	4 + 3 = 7 (odd)
1 + 4 = 5 (odd)	2 + 4 = 6 (even)	3 + 4 = 7 (odd)	4 + 4 = 8 (even)

Math Prompt Checklist

Use this handy checklist to help you keep track of each prompt used throughout the year.

✓	Prompt	✓	Prompt	✓	Prompt	✓	Prompt	✓	Prompt	✓	Prompt
	1		31		61		91		121		151
	2		32		62		92		122		152
	3		33		63		93		123		153
	4		34		64		94		124		154
	5		35		65		95		125		155
	6		36		66		96		126		156
	7		37		67		97		127		157
	8		38		68		98		128		158
	9		39		69		99		129		159
	10		40		70		100		130		160
	11		41		71		101		131		161
	12		42		72		102		132		162
	13		43		73		103		133		163
	14		44		74		104		134		164
	15		45		75		105		135		165
	16		46		76		106		136		166
	17		47		77		107		137		167
	18		48		78		108		138		168
	19		49		79		109		139		169
	20		50		80		110		140		170
	21		51		81		111		141		171
	22		52		82		112		142		172
	23		53		83		113		143		173
	24		54		84		114		144		174
	25		55		85		115		145		175
	26		56		86		116		146		176
	27		57		87		117		147		177
	28		58		88		118		148		178
	29		59		89		119		149		179
	30		60		90		120		150		180

©The Mailbox • *Daily Math Prompts* • TEC60994

Assessment Rubric

Student: _____

Prompt #: _____ Date: _____

Answer:
☐ ☐ ☐
- **2** Answered correctly
- **1** Partial answer given; copied wrong problem; computation error
- **0** Answered incorrectly; no answer given

Understanding:
☐ ☐ ☐
- **2** Understands fully the math needed
- **1** Understands most of the math needed
- **0** Understands little of the math needed

Comments: _____

Explanation:
☐ ☐ ☐
- **2** Communicated ideas clearly
- **1** Communicated ideas fairly well
- **0** Communicated ideas poorly

Comments: _____

Score = ☐

©The Mailbox® • *Daily Math Prompts* • TEC60994

Assessment Rubric

Student: _____

Prompt #: _____ Date: _____

Answer:
☐ ☐ ☐
- **2** Answered correctly
- **1** Partial answer given; copied wrong problem; computation error
- **0** Answered incorrectly; no answer given

Understanding:
☐ ☐ ☐
- **2** Understands fully the math needed
- **1** Understands most of the math needed
- **0** Understands little of the math needed

Comments: _____

Explanation:
☐ ☐ ☐
- **2** Communicated ideas clearly
- **1** Communicated ideas fairly well
- **0** Communicated ideas poorly

Comments: _____

Score = ☐

©The Mailbox® • *Daily Math Prompts* • TEC60994

Prompt Number: _____   Date: _____

©The Mailbox® • *Daily Math Prompts* • TEC60994

Prompt Number: _____   Date: _____

©The Mailbox® • *Daily Math Prompts* • TEC60994